Publication Design by Amanda Jane Jones
Cover photograph by Parker Fitzgerald
Cover Styling by Amy Merrick

weldon**owen**

415 Jackson Street, Suite 200,
San Francisco, CA 94111
Telephone: 415 291 0100
Fax: 415 291 8841
www.wopublishing.com

Weldon Owen is a division of

BONNIER

KINFOLK

SUBSCRIBE

VISIT SHOP.KINFOLKMAG.COM

FOUR VOLUMES EACH YEAR

CONTACT US

If you have any questions or comments,
email us at *info@kinfolkmag.com*

SUBSCRIPTIONS

For questions regarding your subscription,
email us at *subscribe@kinfolkmag.com*

STOCKISTS

If you would like to carry *Kinfolk*,
email us at *distribution@kinfolkmag.com*

SUBMISSIONS

Send all submissions to
submissions@kinfolkmag.com

WWW.KINFOLKMAG.COM

WELCOME

We don't love ice cream because it is good or right or healthy, but because it is not.
Because with ice cream there is no such thing as moderation.
—Nikaela Marie Peters, p. 41

This issue is an ode to ice cream. Much of what we'd like to cover with *Kinfolk* is related to food, community, and the social elements of entertaining, so naturally, ice cream fits as an appropriate theme—few things are as successful at bringing us together. It makes us abandon our differences for the greater, sugary, creamy goodness that it is.

We explore its origins, reminisce about ice cream affairs from when we were kids, introduce a couple that recently started their own ice cream business, and experiment with recipes. We deviate from the theme slightly to share a few spring stories including a seafood harvest (p. 64), coastal biking trip (p. 83), a guide for enjoying the season ("Lessons for Spring" p. 104), and a tongue-in-cheek look at improving our eating habits ("Dietary Confessions" p. 56).

I've had ice cream every day we've worked on this issue, so perhaps it's best if I pass the baton and you take it from here. Crack the spine, sit back, and enjoy this round with a cone or bowl of something cold.

NATHAN WILLIAMS, EDITOR OF KINFOLK MAGAZINE

NATHAN WILLIAMS
Portland, Oregon
Editor

AMANDA JANE JONES
Ann Arbor, Michigan
Designer

DOUG BISCHOFF
Portland, Oregon
Sales & Distribution

JULIE POINTER
Portland, Oregon
Features Editor & Gatherings

KATIE SEARLE-WILLIAMS
Portland, Oregon
Features Editor

PAIGE BISCHOFF
Portland, Oregon
Sales & Order Fulfillment

ERICA MIDKIFF
Birmingham, Alabama
Copy Editor

ANDREW & CARISSA GALLO
Portland, Oregon
Filmmakers

AUSTIN SAILSBURY
Copenhagen, Denmark
Writer

KATIE STRATTON
Dayton, Ohio
Painter

NICOLE FRANZEN
Brooklyn, New York
Photographer

BRITT CHUDLEIGH
Salt Lake City, Utah
Photographer

MARÍA DEL MAR SACASA
New York, New York
Recipe Editor

NIKAELA MARIE PETERS
Winnipeg, Canada
Writer

BÉATRICE PELTRE
Boston, Massachusetts
Chef

AARON WOOD
Melbourne, Australia
Barista

AMY MERRICK
Brooklyn, New York
Stylist & Florist

CHRISTINE WOLHEIM
San Francisco, California
Food Stylist

CLÉMENT PASCAL
San Francisco, California
Photographer

LEELA CYD ROSS
Portland, Oregon
Writer & Photographer

TEC PETAJA
Nashville, Tennessee
Photographer

DANICA VAN DE VELDE
Perth, Australia
Writer

LEO PATRONE
Salt Lake City, Utah
Photographer

CHELSEA PETAJA
Nashville, Tennessee
Stylist

ERIN PROPP
Winnipeg, Canada
Writer

LISA MOIR
San Francisco, California
Stylist

TRAVIS ROGERS
Paris, France
Writer

JASON HUDSON
Toronto, Canada
Writer

LOUISA THOMSEN BRITS
East Sussex, United Kingdom
Writer

CHRIS & SARAH RHOADS
Seattle, Washington
Photographers

JILL LIVINGSTON
Minneapolis, Minnesota
Stylist & Writer

JULI DAOUST
Toronto, Canada
Photographer

WESTON WELLS
Brooklyn, New York
Photographer

JOY KIM
Portland, Oregon
Illustrator

MEGAN GILGER
Traverse City, Michigan
Stylist

WHITEWALL PHOTOGRAPHY
Adelaide, Australia
Photographers

KATHRIN KOSCHITZKI
Munich, Germany
Photographer

NATASHA MEAD
Wellington, New Zealand
Design Assistant

ZACH LIBERTE
Portland, Oregon
Music Composer

KILLEEN HANSON
Portland, Oregon
Writer

NICO ALARY
Paris, France
Writer & Photographer

ALISON WOITUNSKI
Lynn, Massachusetts
Writer

LASSE FLØDE
Oslo, Norway
Photographer

PARKER FITZGERALD
Portland, Oregon
Photographer

ALAN GASTELUM
New York, New York
Photographer

LAURA DART
Portland, Oregon
Photographer

SARAH BURWASH
Nova Scotia, Canada
Illustrator

ASHLEY CAMPER
Maui, Hawaii
Photographer

LAURA FENTON
Brooklyn, New York
Writer

SHEA PETAJA
Traverse City, Michigan
Writer

PAULINE BOLDT
Winnipeg, Manitoba, Canada
Photographer

FEW

ONE

ENTERTAINING FOR ONE

○

THE FARMER'S CANVAS

The patterns and contours of our farmland are a measure of hours and labor.
Each farmer's story is ploughed into the soil.

WORDS BY LOUISA THOMSEN BRITS & PHOTOGRAPHS BY PARKER FITZGERALD

Growing and sharing food binds place and inhabitants together.
Farmers are a bridge between earth and table, seed and sustenance.

We see the fabric of our landscape change with each passing season. Every curve and line, field, and path is shaped by rain, wind, light, footfall, and time. Spring arrives and the seeded furrows, ridges, and folds begin to soften with new growth. Fresh texture and color appear on the farmer's canvas. Fallow months have given them a handful of days to slow down, to listen to the earth, to plant and prepare to meet our needs.

Our farmland is suffused with human feeling. Its patterns and contours are a measure of hours and labor. Each farmer's story is ploughed into the soil. Their livelihood depends on how they till the delicate place between wilderness and man, nature and culture. The wildest part of each of us is our need to survive, to eat, to love, to connect. Growing and sharing food binds place and inhabitants together. Farmers are a bridge between earth and table, seed and sustenance. When we gather to share a meal, we feel our intimate and practical connection with the earth and remember our interdependence.

If we pause to look at the landscape of our own busy lives, to consider what we eat, what we ask for, what we can share, what each of us can bring to the table, we take a step toward a place of careful husbandry and continuous harmony.

When we turn toward the mystery of our own nature, to day and night, season and tide, the rhythm of our instinct and sensations become part of the natural world around us. We give more thought to those whose hands reach into the dark soil to plant at the death of every year and share with them the pleasure and relief of witnessing new growth. Maybe then, we understand that we never really own; we're simply caretakers of a land that reflects our intention, mistakes, and promises.

And so a careful conversation begins between nature, farmers, and ourselves, one that shifts and sighs and assumes the same kind of creaturely life as all the things that grow around us in spring.

Without nature, farmers cannot thrive. They need us to cherish what remains of it and to help foster its renewal. Every spring, theirs is the green hope that we might see, in the pattern of the landscape, the marks of our choices and the tracks we make that are all inextricably linked to the ancient paths that have always connected communities and are still trodden from field to field, from one home to another. ○

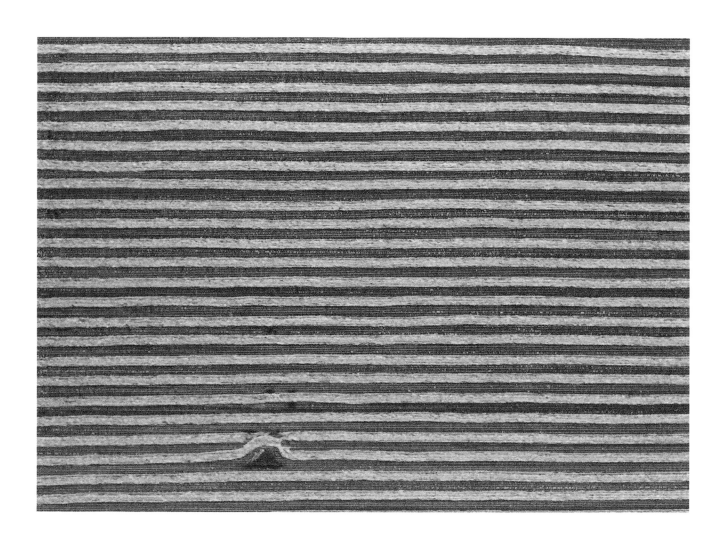

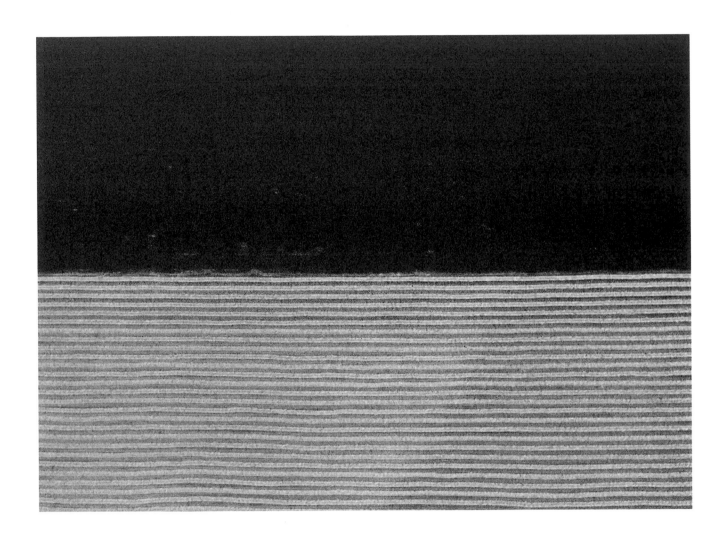

THE PERFECT CUP: AARON WOOD

Amidst a slew of techniques, blends, and brews,
the pleasure of enjoying a cup of coffee can become lost, but Aaron
reminds us that it comes down to simplicity and quality.

A BREWING SERIES BY NICO ALARY

Shooting this photo series with Aaron Wood came at a perfect time. After almost two years I'm packing up my life in Melbourne, and I'm trying to wrap my mind around the idea that next week, I'll be back home in Paris. The timing is perfect because Aaron is one of the very first people I met when I started working in this industry.

I was the greenest barista in town; I was eager to learn, and few people were keen to teach. I got lucky, and eventually I was given the chance to learn from the very talented Talor Browne, who I hope to feature in this series one day. My school was named The Duchess of Spotswood, and there I learned, after many hours of practice (and a fair amount of doubt in my actual capacity to do this job), how to make coffee fast and well.

On Fridays, and on Fridays only, Aaron would be on the bar with me. I instantly liked the guy. I don't think the feeling was mutual. I was a clumsy, slow learner with a French accent and too many questions. But eventually, Aaron and I became really good friends. We shared the same curiosity for the offal cooking happening in the kitchen at "Duchy," and over the months I lived in Melbourne, we shared some brilliant meals, always cooked by him and devoured by me. As I'm on the train from Flinders St. to Kensington, where I'm supposed to meet Aaron, all those memories come back to me and I can't help but smile. Time is a funny thing.

It's a beautiful day; the gorgeous little houses of Kensington look spectacular in the late afternoon light. We set up at the back of the house, in the laneway, in classic Melbourne fashion. Aaron starts brewing the first plunger. He tells me there are two main aspects to a good cup: quality and simplicity. Quality water; quality coffee from a quality roaster; and simple brewing devices, techniques, and instructions. While he's attending the coffee, we talk about how crazy it is that in less than six days I'll be thousands of miles away. We talk about future projects, his upcoming wedding, and his already planned visit to Paris. Two cups of fantastic-smelling Muchai from Kenya are poured and we both quietly sip on it, taking in the soft warmth from the October sun. I think about the fact that I won't be here for summer this year. I think about how much I'm going to miss this city and all the people I met. Coming full circle. Clumsiness is gone, and most questions have been answered, but the accent remains.

AARON'S PERFECT CUP

500 grams filtered water   *15 grams coffee*

METHOD Boil filtered water. Go to the best café you can find and ask if you can get some of their filtered water to compare against your tap water at home.

Use half the hot water (250 grams) to heat your plunger, decanter, and your cups. Place the plunger filter into the water to heat it, too.

Weigh out your coffee. I use a ratio of 6 grams of coffee to 100 grams of water (or 60 grams of coffee per liter of water). Grind your coffee fairly coarse. Your café should be able to show you the best grind for making coffee in a plunger.

Heat remaining water (250 grams) back to boiling. Empty your plunger of its preheated water. Add your ground coffee to the plunger, then add the water. Start timer.

At 3 minutes and 30 seconds, scoop off the crust that has formed at the top, place the filter back on the plunger, and push. Pour ALL the filtered coffee into your empty, heated decanter. Pour into cups as needed, and enjoy. ○

A WAYFARER'S SERIES: LESSONS IN ITALIAN CHERRIES

A visit to an Italian agriturismo *brings an unexpected encounter with the generosity of hosts, the complexities of caring for land, and the good gifts that arise when these two are joined.*

A WORK OF FICTION BY AUSTIN SAILSBURY

PHOTOGRAPHS BY PARKER FITZGERALD & ORIGINAL MUSIC BY LA LIBERTE

ENJOY THIS ORIGINAL SONG WHILE READING THIS STORY

WWW.KINFOLKMAG.COM/LISTEN-ITALY-WAYFARER

These lessons, these treasures found along the traveler's road, can come to the wayfarer in innumerable forms: in the pages of a second-hand paperback, through a spontaneous jump into a jade-green lake, in the words of a rediscovered friend...

It is often true that the best journeys are those full of the unexpected—the surprising and delightful lessons that can only happen because, whether by accident or will, we find ourselves outside the control of our "normal" circumstances. These lessons, these treasures found along the traveler's road, can come to the wayfarer in innumerable forms: in the pages of a second-hand paperback, through a spontaneous jump into a jade-green lake, in the words of a rediscovered friend, or—in the most extraordinary of cases—treasure can be found in the bright red skin and manifold pleasures of fresh Italian cherries.

The first time I traveled through Italy, I was a twenty-one-year-old student: a newly lit match, consuming the old world in a flash of independence and with an unquenchable boyish hunger for all the ancient sweetness of "*la dolce vita*." I traveled light, I traveled rough, and I traveled happily alone. And though that fiery first trip will always hold a special place in my memory, it was thankfully not my last, or even the best, of my journeys into Italy. It was my most recent trip there—a ten-day saunter south from Switzerland to Rome—that has become, unquestionably, the most memorable to me. It was the first trip abroad shared with my wife: a belated European honeymoon navigated with newlywed optimism, a dodgy GPS, and more than our fair share of espresso. This time around I was no longer a backpack-toting, train-jumping, hostel dweller but, just as I had hoped, the journey together was a sweeter one because the memories made, the friends encountered, and the lessons learned were shared.

It was after two in the morning when we arrived at the *agriturismo* I Due Ghiri, and we knew almost immediately that we had stumbled into something wonderful. An agriturismo, in very general terms, is a working farm that takes in travelers as guests. No two are the same. Each has its own charming idiosyncrasies: rustic architecture, livestock roaming freely about, and always the smell of something fresh being baked. Mix in the uncertainty that your hosts will speak English, the treacherous mountain roads to get there, and the relative lack of other tourists in sight, and an agriturismo becomes about as "real" of an Italian experience as a traveler could hope for.

With a smile on his face and an enthusiastically broken brand of English, Stefano—the farmer and owner of I Due Ghiri, who had been waiting up for us to arrive—greeted us. Though it was deep in the night, Stefano met us brightly, and introduced us to our room before bidding us a good evening, just a few hours before he would wake again to begin his work. "In the morning," Stefano promised, "the grand tour, and hot coffee, and a fine breakfast," whenever we decided to wake. Falling into bed like stones, we dissolved into sleep talking about the kindness of our host and how he seemed genuinely glad to meet us—to know us and to have us as guests.

It wasn't until morning that we got a full view of the farm's many splendors and the depth of our host's goodness. Over the next days we learned how much Stefano and his family really did care for all their guests: travelers from the US and Canada, Europe, and Asia. The family, like the farm, was an open door for all; we were instantly befriended and invited inside one of the greatest of all human traditions—the working family farm. On day one, we were tutored in grapes and olives, lectured on coffee and grappa, and most importantly, given a full course on Italian cherries—their varieties, temperament, and proper place in cuisine. I was embarrassed by my ignorance about all things cherry, but Stefano clapped me on the back. "Don't worry," he said, "you will learn many new things in Italy, but we will start with the cherries." We moved

It occurred to me…there is, perhaps, something enlightened in the squinting eyes and the calloused skin of those that work intimately with the land—that they somehow understand the world and their place in it more completely because they have planted and tended and harvested the things that sustain them.

through the sun-kissed grove, examining the hanging blood-red droplets—sampling often as we studied—picking and filling baskets to be pitted the same day for jams and desserts. Never before had we taken such pleasure in produce, never before had we walked and talked with and learned from someone so connected to the land. That week we ate cherries, sour and sweet, with breakfast and from our daypacks and with every meal—cherries we had picked and cleaned ourselves, cherries we had received as gifts from Stefano and the generous earth.

Each night at I Due Ghiri we gathered under the low-arched roof of "the cave" to share a family style dinner with Stefano, his children, and an assortment of other guests staying at the farm. We drank local wines; we ate fresh pasta and roasted chicken, brick-oven bread and *tortelli* shaped by the farmer's talented wife. All of us talked with our hands and toasted our hosts and ate far more than we needed. There, in that cool stone grotto, our motley group became something special—something like a family reunion—newfound friends forgetting, if only for a few hours, that we were strangers.

After dinner, on our last night at I Due Ghiri, Stefano beckoned us out of the cave and onto the terrace for a glass of grappa before bed. Pouring for and "*salud*-ing" us all, he gestured out over the hillside and into the valley. "Look there my friends," he said, inviting our attention away from the house, "the stars up above us and the stars down below." As our eyes adjusted to the night we were amazed to see Stefano's two planes of stars—the familiar constellations above and, down below, millions of fireflies illuminating the valley. In that twinkling silence, looking over the terraced hillside of olive and cherry

trees, I suddenly remembered a college professor who used to say, "All cultures are built on agriculture—it is the source of all our potential." What he meant was that in our common need to be nourished, each of us is connected with one another over the vast spectrum of time—existing somewhere between our grandparents and our grandchildren, we are stewards of the present tense. It is a bond of eternal dependence on the land and the sky and the careful husbandry of seeds and trees and the great living seas. Between the stars above us and the stars below we are but wayfarers all, mere moments in the grand journey of time. We stood there quietly for a long time, drinking the strong fruit, watching a valley full of insects try to compete with the universe, or, at the very least, to get its attention.

It occurred to me, as we said our good–byes the next morning and I shook Stefano's hand a final time, that there is, perhaps, something enlightened in the squinting eyes and the calloused skin of those that work intimately with the land—that they somehow understand the world and their place in it more completely because they have planted and tended and harvested the things that sustain them. In a flashing moment of romance I envied Stefano, his muddy boots, the spade in his hand, and his friendship with the olives and the apples and the bottles of wine that he helped to conceive.

As we drove away, down the dusty grade and through the old farm gate, we took with us baskets of cherries, glowing red in the morning light, but also, a new reverence for the many fine things born in the rich Italian soil and by the sweat of good men and women: another unexpected treasure from the journey, but a treasure all the same. ○

PRACTICAL HANDICRAFT

A CONVERSATION WITH ARIELE ALASKO — INTERVIEW BY JULIE POINTER

PHOTOGRAPHS BY NICOLE FRANZEN

If you have any inclination toward working with your hands, getting a bit dirty, making order out of chaos, your gut reaction to seeing Ariele Alasko's work might be one of regret that you didn't think of it first. Just as soon as this envy creeps in, however, the feeling dissipates into genuine admiration for the thoughtful creations that Ariele crafts with her own two hands, guided by her distinct design aesthetic and the considered desires of her clients. Ariele lives in Brooklyn, New York, where she fills her days with sawdust, making beautiful, practical things out of wood—from cheeseboards to tables to complex wall hangings. After only a few years of making objects of this nature, Ariele's style has become easily identifiable, since her handiwork is largely distinguished by geometric patterns fashioned out of lath—and for those who aren't familiar with timber terms, imagine long, thin strips of wood in varying shades, much like what is used to make a lattice. The use of this humble material reflects the humility with which Ariele fashions these meticulous pieces, making things not for her own pride and glory, but to be used, celebrated upon, and shared by their fortunate owners.

You've mentioned in the past that your favorite thing to make is your lath tables, because it means that you're "building something that people gather around, celebrate on, and are constantly using."¹ How do you see your work as being an integral part of bringing people together? When I was studying sculpture in college, I was constantly having inner battles with the non-functionality of my art. It was perhaps a sign that the match was not made in heaven, sculpture and I, but I continued to struggle with the relationship my entire college career. My mind was always leaning toward making things that would fit in my own home, not in a gallery setting. The moment I pinpointed the problem, I never looked back. It all came down to *function*. I was happiest the day I built a standing cabinet for my kitchen and filled it with things that needed somewhere to go. My answer—that cabinet hinted at—was furniture. And furniture could still be sculpture.

It didn't all fall into place as quickly as that, but that was one moment when I realized that I wanted to build things that people will *use* and everybody needs. When I build furniture for people, tables specifically, I can picture the breakfasts, the dinners, the gatherings they will have around this piece. Most often, a new table is an immediate excuse for a celebratory party, so even right away the table is already doing its part. I love the idea that people can really love a piece of furniture, and it's made even better when that person has a hand in the design process. Every table I build is a specific pattern chosen by that person through a series of sketches and correspondences. In building a table for someone, I'm bringing something into their homes and lives that they will use every single day. That, to me, is so rewarding.

What is the significance for you of being able to eat from, chop food on, work at, sleep under, decorate with, etc. things that you have made yourself? And how much does the anticipated end experience of the piece shape the way you make it? There's an inherent pride that goes into living with something you build yourself. It's in our nature to want to fix, build, beautify, and assemble our surroundings. We've grown so far away from the time when every item we used, and our homes themselves, were something we had to make. As I build a table, it's simply a lesser version of building a cabin from the trees I felled with the axe I forged. Even though I have power tools, I still had to go out searching for the wood and drag it back. When I'm surrounded by all the things I've made in my home, I feel accomplished. I feel like I went outside the normal routine of purchasing-made-easy, and instead, I foraged for materials and worked hard to create whatever it is I need. Obviously I *buy* plenty of furniture as well (mostly from junk stores) but even then it's like a hunt: I go out to the areas where I know I'll have the best shot of finding something, and sometimes you get it, sometimes you don't.

As someone who clearly appreciates handmade things and surrounds yourself with meaningful objects, what is something you truly treasure in your home or studio, and why? Everything in our house has been found or made, for the most part. Our area of Brooklyn was a crazy place for street finds the first five years we lived here, and I would find some treasure on the street at least once a week, ranging from antique oak desk chairs to vintage metal filing cabinets. There are so many pieces we have found over the years that we love even more because we broke our backs hauling them home twenty blocks. We really had to work for it. But perhaps my favorite things in the house are the three metal lamps that my boyfriend and I built together. They are adjustable with bolts and nuts, and are built from found metal that we drilled and cut ourselves. I love them because they are a perfect collaboration between the two of us that we don't often have time for—using his knowledge of kinetics and functionality, and my love for physically putting things together. I'm especially proud of them because each component of the lamps was intended to serve a different purpose before we turned them into lighting, which seems to be a recurring theme in all my work.

Who or what has most influenced your path toward becoming a maker? The interesting thing is that even two years after college I still had no thoughts or intentions of building furniture. I had never done it before, nor did I think about it much, if at all. I became a maker through a jumble of little events that slowly led me toward where I am now. It's hard to pinpoint exactly, but it was almost two years ago that I stumbled across a bundle of lath on the sidewalk. I was walking with my boyfriend, and I picked it up and we brought it home. There was something about it, this little bundle of wood, the way the colors were light on one side and dark on the other, the long thin strips, all uniform in size and length. That bundle sat in our house for a few months until I spontaneously decided to cut it up into little pieces and lay them in a chevron pattern over a larger plank of wood. I didn't have any tools at the time other than a handsaw and a hammer (insane!) so I cut all the forty-five degree angles by hand and nailed them in place with the same nails I pulled from the wood. The result astounded me. The colors were perfection. I rested the two-foot-by-three-foot panel on our mantelpiece and that was essentially how it all began: a lucky find, a sudden idea, a few moments of trying something new, and then it clicked into place.

But the most important thing was a phone call I got a month after spontaneously quitting a sculptor's assistant job. It was my dad on the other line, and he was asking me if I would come to California to build and design his restaurant. Restaurant? A surprise for everybody! He had just stumbled across the perfect space, so spontaneity was a driving force behind many of the next few decisions we made. I started my blog, rented a truck, and drove across the country with a dear friend, Amelie, collecting all sorts of wood and materials along the way (including a huge bundle of lath!). The next seven months of my life were spent building the restaurant, Il Vecchio, entirely from scratch—a hugely pivotal event that changed the entire direction of my life. For one, my patterned tabletops were invented there!

What's been the most surprising thing about this venture you're on—making your own living by building the things you love? When I first graduated college I was in a creative slump. I had no idea what I wanted to do exactly, so I went a normal direction of working for other artists. I was making the ideas of other people come to life, and feeling uninspired to create my own work in general. I couldn't understand how to get inspired and stay that way. When I finally discovered that wonderful thing called lath and began building my furniture, I was stunned at how much inspiration I suddenly had. It came out of nowhere. I was driven, I was excited. I started the blog and people began to find my work and I felt like I was sharing something and connecting with new people. And what has surprised me the most is that I'm able to *stay* inspired—that I've stuck with it even as long as I have and that I keep on going of my own volition. I wasn't sure if I would be entirely capable of self-motivation when left to making all the decisions on my own. Of course, I have my days just like everybody where I don't want to go into work, but mostly I'm thrilled to get to my studio every day. My work is so time consuming, but somehow I'm still enjoying sorting through the same heaps of wood again and again, measuring, cutting, and nailing; measuring, cutting, and nailing, and so on. ○

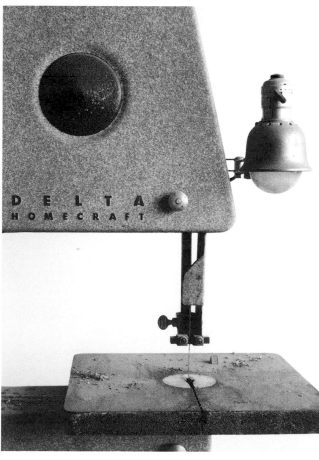

SPRING TRADITIONS

WORDS BY DANICA VAN DE VELDE & ILLUSTRATION BY SARAH BURWASH

Spring immediately conjures up thoughts of new beginnings, fresh growth, and revived ideas. In my romanticized conception of the season, the landscape begins to look like a Claude Monet painting and everything appears to be lighter and in a beautiful state of flux. During this period of transformation, these are the traditions to which I constantly return.

EARLY MORNING BREAKFAST DATES While winter is conducive to the pleasant indulgences of sleeping in and breakfast in bed, the shift brought about by spring demands different morning rituals that involve venturing outside. Waking up early enough to catch the final whispers of birdsong, I love beginning the day with one or two close friends in my regular café. I am a creature of habit, so it is rare for me to order anything other than my preferred combination of poached eggs, crispy bacon, sautéed mushrooms, and sourdough toast. The familiarity of both this dish and the company of friends provides a sense of nourishment that goes far beyond appeasing hunger.

STOCKING THE SPRING PANTRY Both professional chefs and home cooks venerate seasonal cooking, and the benefit of spring is the abundance of fresh produce available. I relish filling my kitchen with fruits and vegetables to create salads, frittatas, and tarts. Basil cut fresh from my potted garden combined with baby *bocconcini*, vine-ripened tomatoes, and a drizzle of olive oil makes for an effortless Caprese salad, while just-picked strawberries gently blended with cream and meringue create a quick Eton mess. Uncomplicated dishes that rely on simple and seasonal ingredients are the essence of my spring repertoire.

IMPROMPTU BICYCLE RIDES As the gray and wet days of the winter months slowly give way to extended hours of daylight and warmth, I most look forward to bringing my bicycle out of hibernation. Her wheels are often flat after months of neglect and her sky-blue exterior usually needs a good dust, but once she has been restored to her former self, it's as though we have never parted. I don't tend to have a specific destination in mind when I set out on my cycling trips; rather, I am content to drift through my neighborhood, observing the everyday life of the season.

AFTERNOON TEA Scones, cucumber sandwiches, vanilla cupcakes, and petite quiches are just some of the items I like on my afternoon-tea menu. Indeed, there is a lovely correlation between dainty and delicate small bites and the lighter appetite inspired by the transition in temperature. Using my

treasured cream porcelain tea set to brew a combination of jasmine tea and rose buds, I love the old-fashioned formality that instantly reminds me of my grandmother. Indeed, the nostalgia of afternoon tea, and the memories it provokes, is a large part of the appeal of this tradition.

PICNIC IN THE PARK Few activities are more evocative of spring than picnics. Although I am a firm believer in placing a blanket and enjoying portable snacks in any available space, there is something to be said for the traditional picnic setting of the park. Whether it is the allure of the environment or the freedom that comes from breaking the routine of housebound dining over the winter, gathering with friends in the park to share food and stories is undoubtedly one of the best ways to pass a weekend afternoon.

THE SPRING MIX For better or worse, spring inevitably brings with it the expectation of spring-cleaning. As a self-confessed neat freak, I am naturally amenable to any excuse to clean clutter and organize my home; however, my pre-cleaning tradition of compiling a spring music mix is what really motivates me to sweep, mop, and polish. I find that the right collection of songs, reminiscent of the season, is ideal to soundtrack all manner of spring activities—whether they be cleaning, baking, or drinking a mid-morning iced tea. This year my cleaning will be set to the sounds of Alpine, Taken by Trees, and Françoise Hardy.

IN BLOOM Following months of bare branches and fallen leaves, a large part of the visual seduction of spring is the first blossoming of nature. While I am sure that most people would love to plant their own garden perfumed with lilacs, ranunculi, peonies, and lisianthus, not everyone has the luxury—or the green thumb, for that matter—to maintain their own flowerbeds. Fortunately, the exterior of my local corner shop is awakened every spring with bouquets of fresh flowers. Admiring the shapes, colors, and textures and choosing a small posy to place in my indoor garden are two of the most special extravagances of the season.

DANS PARIS Now I would never suggest that traveling to Paris for the springtime is one of my traditions; it isn't! More precisely, it is where I would like to spend spring if money and time were not issues. That being said, I do still allow myself to travel by spending the evenings watching my favorite films set in that magical French city. There is something about spring that lends itself to dreaming, and watching Jean-Pierre Jeunet's *Amélie* or Jean-Luc Godard's *Une Femme est une Femme* adds another layer of whimsy to what is already an entrancing season. ○

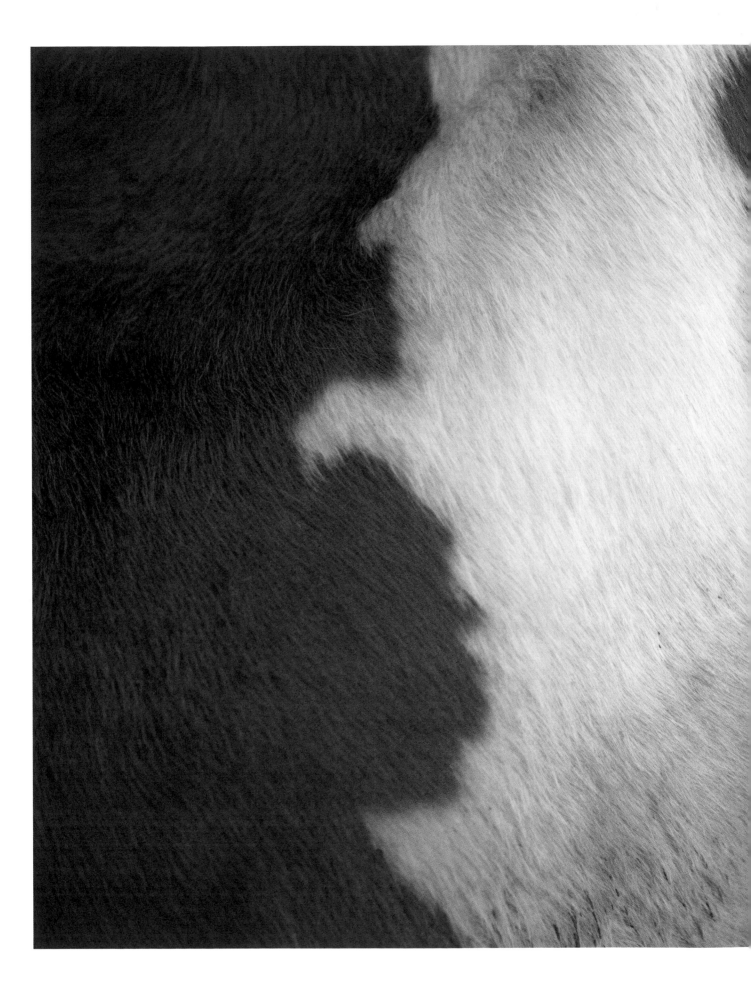

INNOCENT EPICURES: AN ODE TO ICE CREAM

Ice cream, an early love, holds us in its spell long past childhood.

WORDS BY NIKAELA MARIE PETERS & PHOTOGRAPHS BY LAURA DART

ENCOURAGE WHOLESOME DIET

ALLOW PROPER DIGESTION – OBTAIN MILK – EXPRESS GRATITITUDE

CHILL & PROCESS CREAM

One lick reminds you of the whole cone; one spoonful reminds you of the bowl.
You can't save the rest for later. You can't put it in your pocket or hide it in your desk.
Part of the point is to indulge in it—when it is in front of you—now.

From the very start of our lives and the very tips of our tongues, we consume and indulge in milk. It is our first taste. I imagine our taste buds springing into action, tiny tongues awakening. Taste buds were named thus because, according to nineteenth-century scientists, under a microscope they looked like the overlapping petals of a flower. These tongue buds, like their plant namesake, lie dormant in our mouths until they are freed to reach their potential—to blossom into something beautiful; to register a flavor; to bring a pleasure. And the taste buds at the very front of the line, the first buds on the branch, are the interpreters of sweetness. It is no wonder, then, that as soon as we can make a choice, we choose ice cream. As soon as we can speak, we scream. For ice cream.

Perhaps because cream is milk, we love ice cream. But also perhaps because vanilla is an orchid and chocolate is a tree. In other words, there is no rhyme or reason. Maybe the romance is in the fact that it melts—that the days when it is best are the days when its lifespan is shortest. Or maybe we are seduced by the musical trucks that drive down our streets selling it.

There is no addictive ingredient, no caffeine or nicotine, yet we remain transfixed. We don't love ice cream because it is good or right or healthy, but because it is not. Because with ice cream there is no such thing as moderation. One lick reminds you of the whole cone; one spoonful reminds you of the bowl. You can't save the rest for later. You can't put it in your pocket or hide it in your desk. Part of the point is to indulge in it—when it is in front of you—now. Maybe we love the creamy confectionery because it tells us what the ancient Greek philosopher Epicurus told us: that what is pleasureful is what is good and right and healthy.

Epicurus, whose name is synonymous with those who seek pleasure and eschew pain, argued that there is not only an inherent individual benefit to the unnecessary abundances in life, but that there is a lasting and cultural benefit as well. Ice cream, therefore, is good for communities, for the world.

In the small town where my husband grew up, the longest-standing local restaurant is an ice cream parlor. The Hut, which also sells hamburgers and fries, is where you bring relatives when they come to visit. The Hut is where you go after swimming lessons and where you meet

Ice cream is both a time of day and a dessert.
Like tea, it is both a snack between meals and something to finish off dinner.

your friends after school. It's where familiar faces ask how your kids are and about this year's harvest while serving you a double scoop of mint chocolate chip. It is the center of town, a monument to a simpler time.

It might be that no other food or treat could ground a town this way. Ice cream is both a time of day and a dessert. Like tea, it is both a snack between meals and something to finish off dinner. It is a bike ride destination and a marker of the seasons. The Hut closes at the beginning of October, depending on the weather, and doesn't open again till April at the earliest. It's not spring until your first trip to The Hut.

It is surprising that ice cream comes from a recipe, that something that grounds small towns and childhoods and seasons could come from an abstract formula. Most other pleasures we epicures instinctively seek are organic: wine, tea, coffee, sex, sugar, youth. It would almost make more sense if ice cream had been discovered, by accident, like champagne. But, there is a recipe. Ice cream is manipulated into

being. There are egg yolks and specific freezing techniques and lots of whisking. Somehow from this recipe comes our first vice and weakness. Before cigarettes and sangria and crème brûlée, there is ice cream. Long before we fall in love with a human, we fall in love with ice cream. Ironically, when later in life a human breaks our heart, we fall back on our first love. We try to soothe our broken adult hearts by returning to what made our childhood hearts soar: creamy, melting rocky road.

In the 1991 movie *My Girl*, Vada Sultenfuss is instructed to write a love poem. She writes six lines about ice cream. "Wish" rhymes with "dish," "rocky road" with "a la mode." These are the meanderings of an innocent heart. A heart that has not yet known heartbreak or grief. Vada writes an ode to ice cream because, in a way, all kids are epicures. They understand something basic that the rest of us have forgotten: ice cream makes our days happier, which in turn, makes our communities stronger, which, in the long run, makes the world go round. ○

ENJOY

FROZEN GOURMANDS
ILLUSTRATIONS BY JOY KIM

VESSELS / *ceramic, wafer, waffle*

CHILLING TREATS / *gelato, frozen yogurt, ice cream, sorbet*

METHODS / *double bag*

FLORAL SCOOPS

*Whimsical bouquets that appeal to all of the senses
highlight the best offerings of spring.*

PHOTO ESSAY BY PARKER FITZGERALD

STYLING BY AMY MERRICK

DIETARY CONFESSIONS

A parody of common eating idiosyncrasies and the sentences they merit

WORDS BY JASON HUDSON & PHOTOGRAPHS BY LASSE FLØDE

I. PERSONAL DATA			
1. NAME OF ACCUSED (LAST, FIRST) WINTHROP, A.	2. DOB 21 MARCH 1983	3. INITIAL DATE 24 JAN 13	4. TERM 3 Years
II. CHARGES AND SPECIFICATIONS			
5. CHARGE I SECRET EATING: The defendant is charged with hiding away in a car and/or home to eat in secret.	6. SENTENCE The defendant must eat all meals in the brightest light of day, in public, between 11 a.m. and 3 p.m., in the company of other people.		
7. NOTES FROM THE JUDGE Any act that implies shame will be treated as such. Food is to be enjoyed, not consumed secretly in the shadows.	8. JUDGE STEWART, M. 9. JUDGE'S SIGNATURE		

I. PERSONAL DATA			
1. NAME OF ACCUSED (LAST, FIRST) BIRK, R.	2. DOB 02 SEPT 1980	3. INITIAL DATE 3 FEB 13	4. TERM 2 Years
II. CHARGES AND SPECIFICATIONS			
5. CHARGE I EATING IN BED: The defendant is charged with eating crackers in bed.	6. SENTENCE The defendant is charged with 2 years of community service, cleaning the homes of known bed-eaters. The defendant will also be added to the Bed-Eaters Registry, a publically searchable database of these offenders, used primarily by dating websites, to avoid undesirable mismatches.		
7. NOTES FROM THE JUDGE The bedroom is designed exclusively for two purposes: sleeping and reading poetry to your lover.	8. JUDGE ROWMAN, N.		
	9. JUDGE'S SIGNATURE		

I. PERSONAL DATA			
1. NAME OF ACCUSED (LAST, FIRST)	2. DOB	3. INITIAL DATE	4. TERM
DYE, L.	20 MAY 1985	1 FEB 13	1.5 Years

II. CHARGES AND SPECIFICATIONS	
5. CHARGE I	6. SENTENCE
GRAZING: The defendant is charged with eating over the sink in small portions throughout the day.	The defendant must eat three square meals each day, with no nibbling in between.

7. NOTES FROM THE JUDGE	8. JUDGE
Eating while standing is rigorously ill advised. One must always sit, so proper and thorough digestion can occur. And snacks are for children and the weak-willed.	WILLIAMS, N. 9. JUDGE'S SIGNATURE

 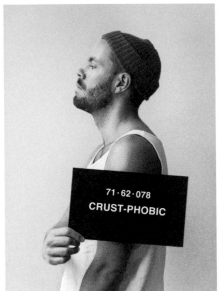

I. PERSONAL DATA			
1. NAME OF ACCUSED (LAST, FIRST) HOLDEN, J.	**2. DOB** 06 DEC 1982	**3. INITIAL DATE** 2 NOV 12	**4. TERM** 18 Months

II. CHARGES AND SPECIFICATIONS	
5. CHARGE I CRUST-PHOBIC: The defendant is charged with flagrant crust removal of the highest degree.	**6. SENTENCE** The defendant is ordered to undergo a strict course of remediation, wherein ONLY the crusts, heels, and stale remains of day-old bread are to be eaten. The defendant will not, for a period of 18 months, be permitted to eat any of the soft, luxurious innards of a loaf.

7. NOTES FROM THE JUDGE Some of the most nutritious aspects of the whole grain can be found in the crusts. They are rich in antioxidants and fiber!	**8. JUDGE** JONES, A.
	9. JUDGE'S SIGNATURE

I. PERSONAL DATA			
1. NAME OF ACCUSED (LAST, FIRST)	2. DOB	3. INITIAL DATE	4. TERM
HAWTHORNE, M.	12 JUNE 1932	15 DEC 12	8 months

II. CHARGES AND SPECIFICATIONS	
5. CHARGE I	6. SENTENCE
KETCHUP–OBSESSED: The defendant is charged with slathering every meal with ketchup.	The defendant is ordered to refrain from ketchup use. However, if the defendant must indulge, the ketchup must be *homemade*.

7. NOTES FROM THE JUDGE	8. JUDGE
Ketchup is not an appropriate topping and should be relegated to children's food. Its sugary consistency is sure to ruin many food items. In rare instances of suitability, ketchup is to be spooned or poured onto the plate, never directly onto food.	HUDSON, J.
	9. JUDGE'S SIGNATURE

TWO

ENTERTAINING FOR TWO

○ ○

SEA HARVEST

*Alison Woitunski reflects on a childhood spent with her father,
the ultimate hunter, gatherer, grower, and lover of food. Alison lives by his example,
and her own relationships—both with her partner and with her food—
reflect this shared love and respect of the coast, passed down from her father.*

WORDS BY ALISON WOITUNSKI & PHOTOGRAPHS BY TEC PETAJA
STYLING BY JULIE POINTER & KATIE SEARLE-WILLIAMS
RECIPE BY BÉATRICE PELTRE

My dad is not a social man, nor is he a still man, and I believe that his need for both solitude and purpose was key in his development as a hunter and gatherer. Never drawn to big woods or large expanses of sea, my dad sought and found his solitude in the small coves and tight inlets of the Northeast Atlantic Ocean, diving for lobsters, crabs, and smaller shellfish, and spear fishing for flounder and bass. In these patches of rocky and intimate waterways north of Boston, my dad honed his hunting and gathering skills. He grew up in a housing project in Peabody, Massachusetts, where neighbors, cars, and electric wires were always a part of his landscape, but in the ocean, those tangible traces of humankind are somehow more subtle, less intrusive. For my dad, his time spent in these places was soulful and productive, as he was always in search of food for his family and peace for himself.

As a child, I learned to view the beaches, waterways, and woods of my region as places where my food came from, and I could taste the differences in what I ate depending on the season or the water temperature. When I was too small to venture into the water alone, I would comb the beach with a milk carton my dad had manipulated into a tool for gathering periwinkles off of the rocks. While my dad was catching the evening's entrée of lobster or crab, I would gather the periwinkles and mussels that would be our appetizer.

I learned to love both the procurement and the preparation of our food. A child of both the sun and the water, I understood innately that the places where these two elements come together are special. It was clear to me what the shoreline could provide, as long as you knew what to look for and where. Back home in our kitchen, my siblings and I would sit around the kitchen table and shuck cooked lobsters for the seafood pie we would eat that night. Taught by our dad how to remove every last bit of flesh from even the tiniest crevices, we extracted meat with a precision and thoroughness worthy of a surgical team. I've never lost this skill and my partner, Bart—a fisherman—claims he knew he was in love the first time he watched me clean a lobster.

That first lobster together was now years ago. As an adult, the places I visited with my father in search of food have become the backdrop for my relationship with Bart. Living on Cape Ann, our days are often spent sailing around the bays and shorelines, with stopovers for free diving, spear fishing, or intentional walks along clam flats. Our equipment might be slightly more sophisticated than my old milk carton, but not by much, and much of it is borrowed from my dad. One of our strongest connectors as a couple is not the actual act of eating together as much as it is our shared enjoyment of the land and water we both grew up with, and have now returned to as adults.

When I remember my childhood meals, taste is an afterthought. Much more vivid is the bustle of our kitchen and our family engaged in the rituals that were employed whenever something living becomes a meal. Whether lobster or deer, there was a process that was both unique and universal and our family hosted its own rules for proper conduct. Ending the day with dinner, my dad would ask, "How is it?" The simplicity of this question acknowledged the routine that this meal was for our family while the act of asking reminded us that what we ate was noteworthy.

Today, Bart and I apply our own processes to our food and how we gather it; some parts are borrowed from childhood and some parts are unique to us. Carried on is the mutual understanding that food from our shores has more significance than just a shared meal.

BUTTER DIP SAUCE

8 tablespoons (4 ounces) unsalted butter
1 tablespoon fresh lemon juice
1 large garlic clove, minced

2 teaspoons fresh tarragon, finely chopped
Salt and freshly ground black pepper
* See metric measurements p. 138

METHOD Melt the butter over medium heat in a small saucepan. Add the lemon juice, garlic, and tarragon and stir until combined. Season to taste with salt and pepper.

Enjoy with crab or lobster tails. *Makes ½ cup.* ○○

CRABBING ESSENTIALS
ILLUSTRATIONS BY JOY KIM

---

1. Gather Your Supplies

  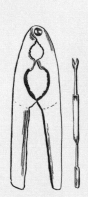 

---

2. Choose Your Net

---

3. Measure Your Crab

The crab must meet a miminum requirement in width to be considered a keeper. Also, most places only allow you to keep the males, which are distinguished by the shape of their narrow abdomen.

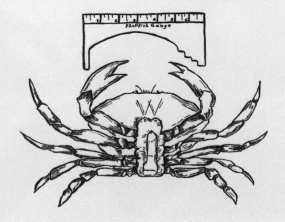

PHIN & PHEBES ICE CREAM

INTERVIEW BY KATIE SEARLE-WILLIAMS & PHOTOGRAPHS BY LEO PATRONE

Phin & Phebes (pronounced "Fin" and "Feebes") Ice Cream is the labor of love of Brooklyn couple Crista and Jess. Phin is short for Phinizy, which is a family name of Crista's. Phebe is Jess's middle name.

The duo made their first batch of ice cream in February of 2010, while pursuing a new wintertime hobby. Their first flavor, Fluffnut—inspired by the Ritz cracker, peanut butter, and marshmallow sandwiches they loved as kids—is now the name of their family dog. Every weekend of the following three months was filled with prototyping and sketching out recipes on the chalkboard wall in their home kitchen.

In January of 2011, almost a year after their Fluffnut batch was created, Jess and Crista did two important things: they attended Penn State's famous weeklong ice cream course, Ice Cream University, and they quit their jobs. With their growing knowledge and overstocked freezer(s), they realized that their hobby was starting to outgrow itself, and they launched their passion into their business, Phin & Phebes.

What do you love most about ice cream? It makes you feel good! If you're sad or had a bad day it can cheer you up. If you're happy it makes you happier. There's an emotional response you have to really good ice cream, you can see it on people's faces—it's just pure happiness. Remember when you were a child and you had that first bite of ice cream and had such an emotional rush? That is why we continue to make ice cream and that is what we believe eating ice cream should feel like.

What brought you into the ice cream business? It really just started as a hobby and we figured out pretty soon that we had an obsession for making ice cream with interesting concepts. There was nothing in the freezer aisle that had clean labels (no stabilizers, syrups, and emulsifiers) that was actually fun and exhilarating to eat. This, combined with our desire to build and make something (this company), kind of sealed the deal for us.

There's an emotional response you have to really good ice cream,
you can see it on people's faces—it's just pure happiness.

How do you come up with new flavors? We tend to eat a lot and we are inspired by foods we are currently eating or lusting over. Usually Jess (Phebes) will bring up some ingredient that she is interested in making an ice cream flavor with, and Crista (Phin) will start blurting out flavor ideas after the brain juices get flowing. From there we prototype our vision in our kitchen until we come up with a flavor we're really happy with.

What's your favorite flavor? This is really hard, because it changes all the time! Jess's sentimental childhood favorite flavor is Black Raspberry and her favorite Phin & Phebes flavor rotates between Vanilla Cinnamon, Vietnamese Iced Coffee, and Banana Whama. Crista's favorite flavor is our Vanilla Cinnamon; clearly she's more decisive on this issue.

What's it like working as a couple? Most of the time it is great, but sometimes it is really hard to not talk about work all of the time and not making that the center of our relationship. I think that any small-business owner would agree that they find it hard to not focus on work all the time. Essentially your business becomes your life, and Phin & Phebes is our life. It's like raising a child, except the child is actually an ice cream company.

What do you see in the future for Phin & Phebes? Our big goal is to change what people think about ice cream with fun, exciting flavors that you can feel good about eating. Even though ice cream is not "healthy," it's one of the purest foods you can eat (if you eat the right ones). We're not entirely sure what the future holds but we're always reevaluating and figuring out the best way to grow as a small company. ○ ○

FEW

ENTERTAINING FOR A FEW

○ ○ ○

SONG OF THE OPEN ROAD

Then and now, ancient and modern, we feel the need to move, to travel, to explore roads both old and new.

EXCERPT FROM SONG OF THE OPEN ROAD BY WALT WHITMAN[3]

PHOTOGRAPHS BY CHRIS & SARAH RHOADS OF WE ARE THE RHOADS

ORIGINAL MUSIC BY LA LIBERTE

ENJOY THIS ORIGINAL SONG WHILE READING THIS STORY

WWW.KINFOLKMAG.COM/LISTEN-OPEN-ROAD

1

Afoot and light-hearted I take to the open road,
Healthy, free, the world before me,
The long brown path before me leading wherever I choose.

Henceforth I ask not good-fortune, I myself am good-fortune,
Henceforth I whimper no more, postpone no more, need nothing,
Done with indoor complaints, libraries, querulous criticisms,
Strong and content I travel the open road.

The earth, that is sufficient,
I do not want the constellations any nearer,
I know they are very well where they are,
I know they suffice for those who belong to them.

(Still here I carry my old delicious burdens,
I carry them, men and women, I carry them with me wherever I go,
I swear it is impossible for me to get rid of them,
I am fill'd with them, and I will fill them in return.)

2

You road I enter upon and look around, I believe you are not all that is
    here,
I believe that much unseen is also here.

Here the profound lesson of reception, nor preference nor denial,
The black with his woolly head, the felon, the diseas'd, the illiterate
    person, are not denied;
The birth, the hasting after the physician, the beggar's tramp, the
    drunkard's stagger, the laughing party of mechanics,
The escaped youth, the rich person's carriage, the fop, the eloping couple,
The early market-man, the hearse, the moving of furniture into the town,
    the return back from the town,
They pass, I also pass, any thing passes, none can be interdicted,
None but are accepted, none but shall be dear to me.

4

The earth expanding right hand and left hand,
The picture alive, every part in its best light,
The music falling in where it is wanted, and stopping where it is not
    wanted,
The cheerful voice of the public road, the gay fresh sentiment of the
    road.

O highway I travel, do you say to me *Do not leave me?*
Do you say Venture not—*if you leave me you are lost?*
Do you say *I am already prepared, I am well-beaten and undenied,
    adhere to me?*

O public road, I say back I am not afraid to leave you, yet I love you,
You express me better than I can express myself,
You shall be more to me than my poem.

I think heroic deeds were all conceiv'd in the open air, and all free
    poems also,
I think I could stop here myself and do miracles,
I think whatever I shall meet on the road I shall like, and whoever
    beholds me shall like me,
I think whoever I see must be happy.

5

From this hour I ordain myself loos'd of limits and imaginary lines,
Going where I list, my own master total and absolute,
Listening to others, considering well what they say,
Pausing, searching, receiving, contemplating,
Gently, but with undeniable will, divesting myself of the holds that would
    hold me.
I inhale great draughts of space,
The east and the west are mine, and the north and the south are mine.

I am larger, better than I thought,
I did not know I held so much goodness.

All seems beautiful to me,
I can repeat over to men and women You have done such good to me I
    would do the same to you,
I will recruit for myself and you as I go,
I will scatter myself among men and women as I go,
I will toss a new gladness and roughness among them,
Whoever denies me it shall not trouble me,
Whoever accepts me he or she shall be blessed and shall bless me.

5

From this hour I ordain myself loos'd of limits and imaginary lines,
Going where I list, my own master total and absolute,
Listening to others, considering well what they say,
Pausing, searching, receiving, contemplating,
Gently, but with undeniable will, divesting myself of the holds that
  would hold me.
I inhale great draughts of space,
The east and the west are mine, and the north and the south are mine.

I am larger, better than I thought,
I did not know I held so much goodness.

All seems beautiful to me,
I can repeat over to men and women You have done such good to me I
  would do the same to you,
I will recruit for myself and you as I go,
I will scatter myself among men and women as I go,
I will toss a new gladness and roughness among them,
Whoever denies me it shall not trouble me,
Whoever accepts me he or she shall be blessed and shall bless me.

6

Now if a thousand perfect men were to appear it would not amaze me,
Now if a thousand beautiful forms of women appear'd it would not
  astonish me.

Now I see the secret of the making of the best persons,
It is to grow in the open air and to eat and sleep with the earth.

Here a great personal deed has room,
(Such a deed seizes upon the hearts of the whole race of men,
Its effusion of strength and will overwhelms law and mocks all authority
  and all argument against it.)

Here is the test of wisdom,
Wisdom is not finally tested in schools,
Wisdom cannot be pass'd from one having it to another not having it,
Wisdom is of the soul, is not susceptible of proof, is its own proof,
Applies to all stages and objects and qualities and is content,
Is the certainty of the reality and immortality of things, and the excellence
  of things;

7

Something there is in the float of the sight of things that provokes it
out of the soul.

Now I re-examine philosophies and religions,
They may prove well in lecture-rooms, yet not prove at all under the
spacious clouds and along the landscape and flowing currents.

Here is realization,
Here is a man tallied—he realizes here what he has in him,
The past, the future, majesty, love—if they are vacant of you, you are
vacant of them.

Only the kernel of every object nourishes;
Where is he who tears off the husks for you and me?
Where is he that undoes stratagems and envelopes for you and me?

Here is adhesiveness, it is not previously fashion'd, it is apropos;
Do you know what it is as you pass to be loved by strangers?
Do you know the talk of those turning eye-balls?

Here is the efflux of the soul,
The efflux of the soul comes from within through embower'd gates, ever
provoking questions,
These yearnings why are they? these thoughts in the darkness why are
they?
Why are there men and women that while they are nigh me the sunlight
expands my blood?
Why when they leave me do my pennants of joy sink flat and lank?
Why are there trees I never walk under but large and melodious thoughts
descend upon me?
(I think they hang there winter and summer on those trees and always
drop fruit as I pass;)
What is it I interchange so suddenly with strangers?
What with some driver as I ride on the seat by his side?
What with some fisherman drawing his seine by the shore as I walk by
and pause?
What gives me to be free to a woman's and man's good-will? what gives
them to be free to mine?

8

The efflux of the soul is happiness, here is happiness,
I think it pervades the open air, waiting at all times,
Now it flows unto us, we are rightly charged.

Here rises the fluid and attaching character,
The fluid and attaching character is the freshness and sweetness of man
    and woman,
(The herbs of the morning sprout no fresher and sweeter every day
    out of the roots of themselves, than it sprouts fresh and sweet
    continually out of itself.)
Toward the fluid and attaching character exudes the sweat of the love
    of young and old,
From it falls distill'd the charm that mocks beauty and attainments,
Toward it heaves the shuddering longing ache of contact.

9

Allons! whoever you are come travel with me!
Traveling with me you find what never tires.
The earth never tires,
The earth is rude, silent, incomprehensible at first, Nature is rude and
    incomprehensible at first,
Be not discouraged, keep on, there are divine things well envelop'd,
I swear to you there are divine things more beautiful than words can tell.

Allons! we must not stop here,
However sweet these laid-up stores, however convenient this dwelling we
    cannot remain here,
However shelter'd this port and however calm these waters we must not
    anchor here,
However welcome the hospitality that surrounds us we are permitted to
    receive it but a little while.

11

Listen! I will be honest with you,
I do not offer the old smooth prizes, but offer rough new prizes,
These are the days that must happen to you:
You shall not heap up what is call'd riches,
You shall scatter with lavish hand all that you earn or achieve,
You but arrive at the city to which you were destin'd, you hardly settle yourself to satisfaction before you are call'd by an irresistible call to depart,
You shall be treated to the ironical smiles and mockings of those who remain behind you,
What beckonings of love you receive you shall only answer with passionate kisses of parting,
You shall not allow the hold of those who spread their reach'd hands toward you.

…

15

Allons! the road is before us!
It is safe—I have tried it—my own feet have tried it well—be not detain'd!
Let the paper remain on the desk unwritten, and the book on the shelf unopen'd!

Let the tools remain in the workshop! let the money remain unearn'd!
Let the school stand! mind not the cry of the teacher!
Let the preacher preach in his pulpit! let the lawyer plead in the court, and the judge expound the law.

Camerado, I give you my hand!
I give you my love more precious than money,
I give you myself before preaching or law;
Will you give me yourself? will you come travel with me?
Shall we stick by each other as long as we live?[3] ○○○

From this hour I ordain myself loos'd of limits and imaginary lines,
Going where I list, my own master total and absolute,
Listening to others, considering well what they say,
Pausing, searching, receiving, contemplating,
Gently, but with undeniable will, divesting myself of the holds that would hold me.
I inhale great draughts of space,
The east and the west are mine, and the north and the south are mine.

— WALT WHITMAN, SONG OF THE OPEN ROAD[3]

SEA—SALTED LEMON ICE CREAM

*Like the blue horizon of the sea, the opportunities that life gives you seem unending.
It is our choice to decide whether to commence on a sour, sweet, or salty path—or whether
to take an adventurous mixture of all three (as suggested by Kathrin's dynamic treat).*

RECIPE AND PHOTOGRAPHS BY KATHRIN KOSCHITZKI

FOR THE ICE CREAM

1 cup (4 ounces) confectioners' sugar

½ cup plus 2 tablespoons (5 ounces) lemon juice from about 3 lemons

3 tablespoons white tequila

2 tablespoons crème fraîche

1 ½ cups (12 ounces) heavy cream

FOR THE SYRUP

Grated zest of 6 lemons

1 ¼ cups (10 ounces) lemon juice from about 6 lemons

½ cup plus 2 tablespoons (5 ounces) water

½ cup (3 ½ ounces) sugar

Coarse sea salt

See metric measurements p. 138

METHOD

Makes 1 pint

1. Stir the confectioners' sugar, lemon juice, and tequila together in a large bowl until the sugar is completely dissolved. Whisk in the crème fraîche and heavy cream, whisking by hand or beating with an electric mixer on medium speed until thickened.

2. Pour the mixture into a 1-pint-/465-milli-liter-capacity container and freeze until solid, at least 3 hours.

FOR THE SYRUP AND SERVING

1. Combine the lemon zest, lemon juice, water, and sugar in a small saucepan and bring to a boil over medium-high heat. Cook, stirring, until the sugar is completely dissolved. Reduce the heat to medium-low and simmer for 3 minutes. Chill completely, about 2 hours.

2. To serve, scatter coarse sea salt on a small plate. Dip the rims of chilled ice cream serving glasses in the syrup, then press them into the salt. Scoop the ice cream into the prepared glasses and drizzle them with syrup to taste. Serve immediately.

SPRINGTIME RENEWAL

TIPS FOR WAKING UP WITH THE SEASON BY ERIN PROPP & TRAVIS ROGERS

PHOTOGRAPHS BY PAULINE BOLDT

Erin Propp's daily life is a testament to the joys reaped from pursuing even the most mundane domestic activities with fresh eyes, intentionality, and disregard for what may be considered modern conveniences. A singer and songwriter by trade, Erin lives in Winnipeg, Manitoba, where the arrival of the spring season is like awakening from the dead. One must take advantage of the slowly lengthening days, the warmer afternoons, the surprise of fresh growth all over again, arriving just when you're sure it will never return. As soon as she can, Erin sets about renewing herself by turning the house inside out, as it were, and making herself at home in the outside world. She and her husband read aloud to each other by an outdoor fire, grow a hearty, shaded garden, and welcome friends and family to join around their open table. In youth, our mothers may have urged us to help with spring-cleaning; now we need promptings toward the personal revival that comes when simple spring tasks are re-examined.

DRY LAUNDRY ON THE LINE. There is something about seeing your work in front of you, hung, clean, fresh, blowing in the breeze, appreciating the industry of wind as it works for you.

READ OUT LOUD. Share a book with your friend or partner and take turns reading out loud to one another. Learn to listen again, to hear the words, like listening to an old radio show.

EAT IN SEASON. Unless you're a canning demon or hunt and salt your own meat, it is very difficult to eat in season in our climate throughout the year. We start more vigorously to eat in-season food in the springtime, making a weekly trip to a home-grown market. This changes my regular shopping route, is usually more expensive, and makes me change my recipes, but it also forces me to slow down, consider what we are putting in our bodies, and oftentimes I meet new people in the new places I end up in. I don't even think of it in those terms—I just love going to my favorite markets when they finally open in May and June.

PLANT A GARDEN. The time spent getting to know seeds, soil, and even self in the garden is a worthwhile pastime. Most-used growth: scant strawberries and raspberries for toppings on baked oatmeal and desserts, and basil and rosemary for pizzas and roasts.

HELP A CHILD. Labor plus nature equals capital for our souls, minds, and hearts. Invest in something important by helping a child (perhaps your own) with his or her homework. Because let's be honest—algebra is as rooted and indecipherable in our own lives as are the stars in the sky.

CLEAN YOUR HOME. On the first warm Saturday, grab a broom and sweep out all large closets, the garage, and other storage areas. You'll find space, and perhaps treasured photos and keepsakes you forgot you had. Your home is part of your memories, your stories, and your life. Explore it a bit.

DANCE. Take the bicycle or motorcycle out for a nice ride in the still-chilly morning air; take a walk after dinner to notice the return of creatures small and large, and the flowers beginning their growth from underground, in fantastic intimacy. Spring is a return to motion for all.

BRING THE OUTSIDE IN. Put some small potted flowers in favored spots around the house or apartment; it's a great way to add instant color and, quite literally, the smell of spring.

VISIT A NEIGHBOR. Some move away; others move in next door and sing opera at one in the morning—all the more reason to bring a small gift and a smile. At the very least, you can cultivate a friendship and sing opera together.

TRY NEW FOOD. Infuse new recipes into your kitchen for the year. Consider starting with a dessert, because frankly, chocolate and its sweet cousins are kings of the world. Try this French-originated dish: *tarte aux figues* (fig tart). Make or purchase a large thin pastry crust, top with fig jam, then with sliced fresh figs. Sprinkle generously with sugar and melted butter, and then brush the edges of the crust with one egg yolk. In 30 minutes at a medium heat you shall have a tasty and simply made dessert, to inspire a year of satisfyingly rich dinner-table memories. ○ ○ ○

HOW TO BE NEIGHBORLY: CHECKING IN

We've all received that out-of-the-blue note from a friend; the joy and comfort that these little check-ins bring us is incredible considering the simplicity and scale of the act. It doesn't take much time or effort to jot down a thinking-of-you note to a friend that will change their day.

A woman once received a letter from a dear friend who was traveling far from home. He was sitting in the airport bar, the man wrote, waiting for his flight, and a young girl had just walked by. She reminded him of the woman. She had the same eyes, the man wrote, the same smile, the same face. She looked just as the woman had when she was young.

The letter was written on a cocktail napkin from that airport bar, folded hastily into an envelope, and licked shut with a two-penny stamp. It wasn't anything particularly special. It wasn't full of details or professions of affection. Rather, it was a small, two-penny reminder written on a cocktail napkin: simple proof that he had been thinking of her. The man didn't add the letter to his to-do list. He didn't delay because he had to meet someone for dinner, or until he had a spare hour or two to devote to the task. This was simply one letter among many, part of a quotidian, unaffected habit of letting people know they were thought of.

This scene, from *Charming Billy* by Alice McDermott[4], has lingered with me over the years since I first read it. In comparison to that letter-writer, I'm guilty of long to-do lists and of putting things off so I can do them "right." There is a small pile of letters on my desk that I have yet to respond to, one from an embarrassing thirteen months ago, because I want to write a "proper" letter. By that, I mean the kind that I imagine nineteenth-century correspondents might have exchanged. It's an unfortunate cycle: the longer they sit unanswered, the more pressure I feel to make the response special. This, then, means they'll sit on my desk still longer.

Two-penny letters are like drops of water into buckets. Over time, one hopes, those buckets become full, saturated. We know that relationships of all kinds need regular check-ins. Too infrequently and it's hard to make much progress. The friendship drifts. The water evaporates. Neither will be as full as they might have been.

My parents are both inveterate letter writers. Every week, almost without fail, I receive a letter from one or the other of them, full of clippings from the local hometown paper, old drawings of mine from elementary school, or twenty-dollar bills for gas money, though I'm long past asking to borrow the family car. Their letters are not particularly photogenic or calligraphic. My father's letters come on old business letterhead. My mother, though you'd never guess it, is a pro at steaming open junk mail envelopes and stashing her own notes and clippings inside before forwarding them on. Their messages are often only a paragraph or two, just long enough to share a quick anecdote. I'm glad to know that they think of me. They've filled my bucket to overflowing.

I'm trying to live up to their example. I'm personally a big fan of postcards and sticky notes. It's the simplest thing to jot "What a lovely garden," on a postcard and tuck it in a neighbor's front door. Or to write "Love this!" and stick a note to a work-in-progress on someone's studio table. "Hi friend. Coffee soon?" is another good one. I collect postcards at cafés, at bookstores, and at flea markets. Because they're often free and quirky, they can prompt great messages. And because the space for text is so limited, there's no pressure to write something especially weighty or profound. Instead, you simply tell someone that you were thinking of them. That they were on your mind, even amidst the day's hustle. If you add a stamp, that's more to the better. Everyone loves mail.

My parents are proof that there's no excuse, not when it's so easy, for not telling someone you're thinking of them. If it occurs to me that I haven't talked to Silas recently, or that I ought to invite Lilah to dinner, it's as simple as a sentence or two. For those more digitally inclined, it can be a quick text message or email. I save each and every letter I receive. There are years of them in my closet. What blessings.

WORDS BY KILLEEN HANSON & PHOTOGRAPHS BY BRITT CHUDLEIGH

LESSONS FOR SPRING

*Spring, like the age-old sayings go, is a time for fresh starts and trying new things.
Let these words and photos be a starting place as you begin your own pursuit of change.*

WORDS BY JULIE POINTER & PHOTOGRAPHS COMPILED BY AMANDA JANE JONES
PHOTOGRAPH CREDITS LISTED ON P. 138

LEAVE THE INDOORS BEHIND

CHOOSE A NEW HOBBY

DON'T BE IN SUCH A HURRY

TAKE MATTERS INTO YOUR OWN HANDS

REAWAKEN YOUR YOUTH

SIT IN SILENCE, ALONE

DRAW CLOSE TO THOSE NEAREST AND DEAREST

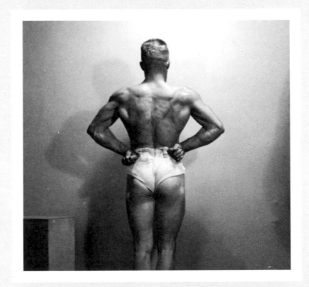

DON'T MIND BEING ECCENTRIC

FALL IN LOVE WITH SOMETHING NEW

DIVE IN DEEP

FARMERS BEHIND THE MARKET

WORDS BY LAURA FENTON & PHOTOGRAPHS BY WESTON WELLS

In New York City, spring arrives later than you might think. Each April, the weather softens, crocuses push up from the ground, and trees break into blossom, but it'll still be weeks before the first asparagus arrive at the market.

Opened in 1989, the farmer's market at Brooklyn's Grand Army Plaza connects farmers to city residents, including many families, who arrive from the adjoining neighborhoods of Park Slope, Prospect Heights, and Crown Heights.

Through the early spring, twenty-six vendors brave the cold: farmers sell potatoes, root vegetables, and apples; the flower vendor stocks dried blossoms; and dairy farmers continue to peddle their cheeses. Devoted market shoppers will appear each week no matter what the season, but it is in spring when the market comes back to life—both in the stalls and in the community. Spring's fiddlehead ferns, spring onions, ramps, and rhubarb are treasured arrivals for the chef of any stripe.

The market at Grand Army Plaza is more than a place to buy produce. Shoppers will find dairy, maple syrup, pickles, grains, cheese, wine, and more. Greenmarket, the nonprofit that operates the market, also offers food scrap collection for composting and textile recycling. The market is the hub of the local food movement, and in the spring, it is our connection to the first stirrings of new life on farms that surround the city.

NO. 1 Filmmaker Anna Rose Holmer has been selling flowers for Lebak Farms for the past two years. While she lives in Bedford-Stuyvesant today, Holmer worked for a CSA before moving to New York City.

NO. 2 Raymond Bradley of Bradley Farm in New Paltz, NY, rises at 2:30 in the morning in order to pack up his produce for the Saturday market. Bradley has always had strong ties to food: prior to becoming a farmer, he was a chef for thirteen years.

NO. 3 Kendra Lewis started working the Bradley Farm stand in July of 2012, but on weekdays she is working on her master's degree in education at Bankstreet Graduate School.

NO. 4 For two years, Brooklyn resident Rich Allium has managed the booth for Blue Moon Fish. The local fishing operation is based out of Mattituck, NY, which lies ninety miles east on the north shore of Long Island.

NO. 5 Author Robin Shulman visited the Grand Army Plaza market to promote her book *Eat The City: A Tale of the Fishers, Foragers, Butchers, Farmers, Poultry Minders, Sugar Refiners, Cane Cutters, Beekeepers, Winemakers and Brewers Who Built New York*.

NO. 6 Lynn Fleming's dairy farm, Lynnhaven Farm, is based in Pine Bush, NY. Fleming has been selling her goat cheeses, goat meat, and eggs at Grand Army Plaza for seven years, and in that time, she says, "I have friends here, and I have seen their children grow up."

NO. 7 Liz MacAlister is the proprietor of Cato Corner Farm, a dairy farm with ninety head of cattle in Colchester, CT. MacAlister has been farming since 1979 and working the Grand Army Plaza market since 1999. All of Cato Corner's cheeses are made from raw milk and aged for at least sixty days.

NO. 8 Bill Maxwell was among the handful of vendors who sold their produce at the Grand Army Plaza market when it opened more than twenty years ago. His farm, Maxwell Farm, is located in Changewater, NJ, about eighty miles due west of the city. Maxwell, a former newspaper reporter, fell into farming when his own vegetable garden got so big that he decided to sell some of his excess produce.

NO. 9 Over the years, Karen Young has worked many booths at farmer's markets. She started with Phillips Farms and spent a few years with Blue Moon Fish; today, she works for Liz MacAlister of Cato Corner Farm. When she's not at the market, Young is a visual artist and sculptor. ○○○

THE ALCHEMY OF A GOOD MEAL

INTERVIEW BY SHEA PETAJA & PHOTOGRAPHS BY TEC PETAJA

STYLING BY CHELSEA PETAJA

We live on a sizeable peninsula known as the "pinky" of Northern Michigan, surrounded by big lakes and lathered with little ones. We live here by choice, not default, and share a mutual respect for this decision. The four seasons move in and out of our area without permission and we move with them. We call ourselves Northerners and with this title we are claiming land, stretching our vocational abilities, and learning to love each other in towns with little elbow room. I hesitate to call us scrappy. I prefer to use the word "resourceful." Case in point: Andy Schudlich and Cammie Buehler, co-conspirators of Epicure Catering & Cherry Basket Farm. These two friends met years ago as transient twenty-somethings working the local kitchen scene with no intention of settling. As the years rolled on and their lives took shape, it became obvious that given their creativity and connections, something magical would happen. And it did.

Cherry Basket Farm, which also houses Epicure Catering, is situated around the bend in Omena, a small but mighty town even farther up the pinky. Many farms in this area are threatened by development and this farm was no different—it was on the subdivision chopping block before Cammie's parents snatched it up. The original five buildings stand tall as if they were predestined for their current purpose: to house epicures. And while most events are for strangers (can you call Chef Mario Batali a stranger?), we the locals—the Northerners—partook in its glory one evening.

Before our gathering, I meandered around Cherry Basket Farm, building by building, soaking in the history and wishing I could hear the walls speak. I snuck into the white board-and-batten kitchen house, and inside I found Andy working his alchemic chef magic. Smoke from the fire pit outside drifted in, the smell building anticipation. A local Native American fisherman had brought Andy a walleye from the lake that morning and Andy had plans to bake it in a salt cocoon over the fire. The salt would harden like concrete, allowing the flavors to soak into its flesh.

As I watched him whisk the salt I asked, "What recipes do you use?" He replied, "Recipes? There are no recipes. It's more like, 'That's not sticky enough, it needs more water,' so I add it." His kitchen help spoke up, "I'm just glad there is a hammer involved!" I didn't understand, and Andy wouldn't confess; he's a culinary prodigy with many legendary secrets. A mutual friend leaned into me later that evening and said, "Did he tell you about the time they were swimming in Lake Leelanau? Andy spent the whole day collecting clams from the bottom of the lake, brought them to shore, cooked them on a fire he built, and flipped over kayaks to use as tables." I laughed: there are no edible clams in Lake Leelanau, but there are legends and evenings spent eating over kayak dinner tables.

As the sunset and the lake breezes drifted across the farm, I took a deep breath of the good life. Under the canopy tree sat twenty people ready to partake in the talent of Andy and the fortitude of Cammie. A parade of goodness began, and with each plate presented, the decibel of the conversation dropped. Cammie broke the silence. "Wow. I think we have enough!"

At the table that evening, we embraced the splendor of food and friends before us. The candles flickered in applause. Our table was tucked in between barns and next to an orchard. These were our friends and this food was our pleasure. What Andy and Cammie were able to create from their land and the land we claim as Northerners brought us together. Each of our contributions was being shared and we passed the goodness around. I glanced over to see Andy grin. Perhaps he knew something we didn't, or perhaps this was another story being tucked away for the keeping.

You're different from other caterers; why? Cammie: We are the only fine dining, local food caterer in this area. We don't have a restaurant on purpose. In addition, we only do one event at a time…. It is a completely comprehensive service. We find our food locally and we find the career staff. Andy and our staff make the food onsite. If the event is in the middle of a field, then we bring our entire kitchen out to that field. It was a nightmare in the beginning but now it's controlled chaos.

Most caterers prepare food in advance and take it to the event. You don't; why? Andy: Why? Because it's better to cook at the event. We do it because it's right, not because it's easier. The food smells better and it tastes better. Guests get to smell the food as it cooks and the immediacy of the preparation makes it taste better. At any event,…you want that.

C: Your menu choice, procurement of materials, and attention to detail should be on par with the amount of the detail given to the other parts of the [event], such as the decor, for example, or your guest list.

Did you ever think you'd be doing this ten years after starting? C: This business started as a lifestyle choice. We wanted to cook using local goods, we wanted to do a good job and…we had no idea it would take off. When we started this business, very few people in the area were using locally grown food. It would take us an entire day to gather the food for one event.

A: It took me eight hours to gather for one event. Ten years later and we have refined the gather time down to two to three hours per event. There are more infrastructures in the local food community now;…the network has grown and consumption of local foods has grown. Consumers as well as chefs are seeking local items and because of this, they are more readily available. This is a national movement, and Michigan, being such an agricultural bastion, is right in step.

Why have you chosen to stay in Northern Michigan? C: Northern Michigan is one of most diverse and viable agricultural areas in the nation. We have been taking advantage of this and supporting local farmers. Each event requires a new menu made entirely of local goods. For example, I would love to make food with avocados, but we simply don't because they aren't grown here.

No recipes? A: No. If you use good products and mess with them as little as possible then you get the best results. There are no cutting corners. Bad meat and bad produce make it harder to cook.

How do you celebrate the end of the season? C: We have a friends gathering at the Farm. It is a way for us to come up for air and say "hi" to our friends and celebrate the good season and to thank them for supporting us.

A: <insert Andy's grin> It's fun to see some of our clients who have become friends hanging with the cooks and the locals. Everyone is together and it's a really neat experience.

What do you want people to take away from this interview? A: Do a good job. Don't just do a good job based on the client's expectations; do better. Exceed what you know as good. We cook as if we are cooking for friends, with the utmost care. [Because] we only do one event at a time, we can focus on the people we have the privilege of cooking for. ○○○

GOAT TOWN'S CHAMOMILE ICE CREAM

INGREDIENTS

1 cup (12 ounces) honey

2 tablespoons dried chamomile flowers

4 cups (32 ounces) heavy cream

4 cups (32 ounces) whole milk

¼ cup (1.2 ounces) dry milk powder

Metric Measurments

340 grams honey

2 tablespoons dried chamomile flowers

945 milliliters heavy cream

945 milliliters whole milk

35 grams dry milk powder

METHOD

Makes 1 quart

1. Stir the honey and chamomile together in a large saucepan and cook over medium-high heat, stirring occasionally, until the mixture begins to bubble. Reduce the heat to medium and cook for 3 minutes.

2. Wrap a damp towel around the base of a large bowl to steady it on a work surface. Pour the cream into the bowl, then pour the honey into the cream in a slow steady stream. Return the mixture to the saucepan and stir in the milk. Cook the mixture over low heat just until it begins to simmer.

3. In a small bowl, stir the milk powder and 1 cup of the heated cream mixture until completely dissolved. Add the mixture to the saucepan, stirring to combine. Strain the mixture back into the bowl through a fine-mesh sieve (discard the solids) and cool to room temperature. Cover the bowl with plastic wrap and refrigerate until completely chilled, at least 2 hours.

4. Churn the mixture in an ice cream maker according to the manufacturer's instructions. Transfer it to a 1-quart-/950-milliliter-capacity container (or two 1-pint-/465-milliliter-capacity containers) and freeze until set, 1 to 2 hours. Serve.

Recipe by Goat Town
Photographs by Alan Gastelum

FLOWER POTLUCK

WORDS BY AMY MERRICK & PHOTOGRAPHS BY PARKER FITZGERALD

F riends, flowers, food. Is there really anything more? Raise your springtime serotonin levels by gathering a group of your favorite people for a flower-arranging potluck and lunch. If each person brings a bunch of flowers and a snack to share, celebrating the season's newfound warmth will be a breeze.

NO. 1 In the same way that you want a mix of mains, sides, appetizers, and drinks at a potluck, the floral materials should be equally as varied. Friends should bring a single bunch of one type— branches, flowers, foliage, a case of mason jars, or a handful of garden shears.

NO. 2 Create an arranging buffet. Each variety should be organized in its own vase or bucket. Label with the name if you feel fancy. (Not feeling fancy is okay, too.)

NO. 3 Embrace mismatched colors and wild, foraged materials. Have fun and arrange loosely! Flowers look the prettiest when they seem to be growing out of the vase, so try not to cram them.

NO. 4 Remember to cut stems at an angle and remove leaves from below the waterline. Change the vase water daily for the longest show.

NO. 5 Flowers can be found anywhere. The farmer's market, local nursery, grocery store, your backyard, or the side of the road are your best bets for a good deal.

NO. 6 Arrange first and eat after. Sweep off the table when it's time for lunch but don't bother with the stems on the floor. A pretty mess is to be savored. Set the table with your finished bouquets and enjoy together. ○○○

LOS ANGELES / TORONTO / PARIS

WORDS BY JULIE POINTER

On the brink of autumn, we convened in the Arts District of downtown Los Angeles at Apolis: Common Gallery for an evening spent enjoying the last fruits and flavors of summertime. Strung around the room were vestiges of the past season's bounty, including herbs, hops, persimmons, olive branches, and foliage that fragranced the room. We welcomed winemakers, designers, photographers, doctors, architects, sociologists, makers, and more around the table, and enjoyed a lively night of good conversation and decadent food. The making of this dinner was particularly collaborative in nature, and we were honored to share the night with so many new and old friends within the ranks of our growing community. *Photographs by Leo Patrone (top two and second spread)*

Our gathering in the town of Tiny on the Georgian Bay of Ontario, Canada, was a welcome midsummer escape for Toronto dwellers. A small group of makers, chefs, artisans, shop owners, and photographers converged at a lakeside cottage for an entire day, with only the conviction set before us to enjoy one another's company and to eat well. We prepared food together, swam, lounged on the deck, wilted in the heat, and feasted—three separate times. The occasion proved rightly that experiences shared and tasks enacted together—even over the course of a mere day—lay the groundwork for lasting relationships and the tying of common bonds. Hesitant strangers in the morning were friends breaking bread around the table by dinnertime. The day was made complete by the generous provisions of both those local to the Bay and to Toronto, ensuring that we had enough baked goods, chocolate, cheese, fish, and fresh produce to last us days at the water's edge—if only we had been so lucky. *Photograph by Mjölk*

A picnic on the banks of the Seine in Paris, France, confirms that the most low-key of gatherings can result in something wonderful and unimagined, if planned with the right mixture of forethought and room left for spontaneity. A small group of picnickers descended upon the riverbank just across from the Eiffel Tower, for a fresh summer spread of goods from some of the best local purveyors. There was no fancy table, vintage silverware, or expensive glassware—instead, just blankets stretched across cobblestone, bikes propped askew, and paper plates piled with the season's offerings. Once again, the warm spirit of those gathered superseded the need for an extravagant setting, as diners lingered long into the evening, brought together for the simple act of sharing a meal, conversation, and enjoying the plenitude of their shared city. *Photograph by Clément Pascal* ○○○

KINFOLK DINNER SERIES
LOS ANGELES 2012

MENU

Passed Hors D'oeuvres
Honey Fig & Plum Bruschetta
Pumpkin Tacos
Pickled Shrimp

On the Table
Fresh Baguettes & Preserved Lemon Dip

First Course
End of Summer Salad

Second Course
House Cured Salmon with Cardamom & Lemon Verbena

Family Style Dinner
Braised Pork
Heirloom Tomato Tart
Caramelized Corn with Buratta

Dessert
Lemon Rosemary Cake

PARTNERS

Apolis Global	Type A Press
West Elm	Handsome Coffee Roasters
The Paper Palate	Rachel Craven
Three Sticks Winery	Dovetail
Peddler's Creamery	Twig & Twine
Winiful	Leo Parrone
Cookbook LA	Anja Mulder
Moon Juice	Greenbar Collective
Yeah! Rentals	Casa De Perrin
	Brakeman Brewery

LIFE ON THE LAKES

*Minnesota's abundance of lakes play an important role
in the lives of those who live nearby.*

WORDS AND STYLING BY JILL LIVINGSTON

PHOTOGRAPHS BY ASHLEY CAMPER

Amid the dynamic energy of a modern city, the Minneapolis Chain of Lakes remains a quiet and verdant core. This is a place where we feel at ease to gather and explore, to relax and play. Lakeside and water trails are an engaging alternative to concrete paths and roads. Boats are platforms from which to dive and swim far from the shoreline. The middle of the lakes offer a unique vantage point from which to view the growing city. Young couples push off at dusk to drift off into the darkness alone on their crafts and in the night. Life on the lakes is one of novelty and freedom, and Minneapolitans embrace it.

In the earliest days of spring, we are eager to come together once again on the water. With woolen blankets and thermoses full to fight off the spring dawn chill, we portage our canoes from car roof to shoreline. A short paddle brings our flotilla to a favorite spot along a canal where we anchor and enjoy the first fruits of the season. Wild mushrooms and ramps give a distinctly earthly tone to quiche, and rhubarb jam brightens brioche. We have been here before but each time feels exciting and new. Experiencing even the most simple acts of life on the lakes makes each movement more acute and each moment sweeter. ○ ○ ○

This is a place where we feel at ease to gather and explore, to relax and play.

———————————————————————————————————————

—JILL LIVINGSTON

NATURE'S SALT

INTERVIEW AND PHOTOGRAPHS BY LEELA CYD ROSS

Wind brushes, cold and biting, no matter the time of year, turning cheeks a vivid pink. The only sounds to be heard: sea gulls' light touch down on the empty beach and the gentle sloshing of water in a bucket. The elements are what originally drew Ben Jacobsen, of Jacobsen Salt, to start creating salt from Netarts Bay water on the northern Oregon Coast several years ago, and it's the natural elements that keep his business and spirit going. Ben's the only person making hand-harvested salt in the Pacific Northwest. Chefs and home cooks love his product because of its mineral flavor and locality. When sitting down to a meal of backyard produce, wines from next door, butter from a nearby farm, and bread fresh from the oven, the thing to set off each and every bite? A hearty fingertip pinch of fresh, natural salt from the briny sea by way of Ben Jacobsen.

What inspired you to first start harvesting salt? Really just curiosity at first. I love great salt, and I wanted to figure out how to make my own. I thought that if salt could be harvested in the UK where Maldon is from, it must be possible right here in Oregon.

How does working on the Oregon Coast affect your life? It's grounding. Pickup trucks, cows, agriculture, fishing boats are a way of life on the Oregon Coast. The harsh and oftentimes tough elements also really make you beautiful days. That said, I love the dark, cold, rainy, and windy days just as much as the sunny days. The tough days build character.

What do you say to folk who think you're crazy? The first company in Oregon to harvest salt since Lewis and Clark? Definitely either crazy or genius. I love what I do and I'm proud of the product we create. I just hope there are a few people each day who our product and brand resonate with, and hopefully those will outweigh the people who think we are crazy. I guess I do have a little crazy in me as well.

What's the ideal item to sprinkle your salt upon? Everything! That's the great thing about salt. I have it on toast and eggs almost every morning. You can mix our salt into a vinaigrette to add a delicate briny crunch to your dressing. You can add it to grilled meat, vegetables, and really nearly anything to add a nice bit of contrast and flavor to whatever it is you are cooking. I also like to put it on ice cream as a special treat. ooo

FRESH LIME AND JASMINE TEA

INGREDIENTS

3 limes

3 cups (24 ounces) limeade, chilled

2 cups (16 ounces) brewed jasmine green tea, chilled

1 cup (8 ounces) cold water

2 teaspoons finely grated zest plus ¼ cup (2 ounces) freshly squeezed lime juice from about 4 limes

Sugar

Ice cubes

See metric measurements p. 138

METHOD

Serves 4

1. Cut one of the limes in half lengthwise; set aside. Slice the remaining two limes into thin rounds (you may freeze these into ice cubes, if desired).

2. Combine the limeade, tea, water, lime zest, and lime juice into a medium-sized pitcher and stir until combined. Add sugar to taste. If you did not freeze the lime slices into the ice cubes, add the slices to the pitcher.

3. To serve, scatter sugar on a small plate. Use one half of the reserved lime to rub the rims of 4 glasses and press them into the sugar.

4. Fill the glasses with ice, and serve the tea-limeade. Use the remaining lime half to add an extra hit of lime flavor, if desired. Serve immediately.

Recipe by Katie Searle-Williams
Photographs by WhiteWall Photography

ANTIQUATED

Elbows on the table are admissable between courses, but not while eating.

A spoon should be placed in the saucer if more coffee or tea is desired.

Mixing food on the plate is in bad taste.

Food & utencils should not be played with.

Let food be taken to the mouth, not mouth to the food.

Noises should not be made while eating.

ENDURING

Do not talk with food in your mouth; chew with your mouth closed.

Eat bites that are manageable for your mouth size.

Refrain from picking your teeth at the table.

Avoid slouching & resting your limbs on the table.

Say "excuse me" when you leave the table during the meal.

Say "please" & "thank you."

SPECIAL THANKS
Paintings Katie Stratton
Art Director at Weldon Owen Ali Zeigler
Production Director at Weldon Owen Chris Hemesath
Partnership with Kodak

Kodak

PROFESSIONAL Products

SEA HARVEST
Location Kelly's Brighton Marina *kellyscrabs.com*

Butter Dip Sauce (Metric)
113 grams unsalted butter
45 milliliters fresh lemon juice
1 large garlic clove, minced
2 teaspoons fresh tarragon, finely chopped
Salt and freshly ground black pepper

SONG OF THE OPEN ROAD
Wardrobe & Props Lisa Moir
Food Styling Christine Wolheim
Makeup/Hair Renee Rael
Locations Outerlands & Central Kitchen in
San Francisco

SEA-SALTED LEMON ICE CREAM (METRIC)
120 grams confectioners' sugar
150 milliliters lemon juice from about 3 lemons
40 milliliters white tequila
50 grams (1.8 ounces) crème fraîche
350 milliliters heavy cream
—
For The Syrup
Grated zest of 6 lemons
300 milliliters lemon juice from about 6 lemons
150 milliliters water
100 grams sugar

LESSONS FOR SPRING
Leave the Indoors Behind
Reprinted with permission. Department of Maps, Prints and Photographs, The Royal Library, Denmark. *Young people at the beach*, Sven Türck (1897-1954).

Choose a New Hobby
Courtesy of the Library of Congress, Prints & Photographs Division, FSA/OWI Collection, LC-USW3- 029809-E. *Arlington Cemetery, Arlington, Virginia. A girl taking a picture of the ceremony of laying a wreath on the Tomb of the Unknown Soldier (LOC)*, Bubley, Esther, photographer, 1943 May.

Don't Be in Such a Hurry
Reprinted with permission. Department of Maps, Prints and Photographs, The Royal Library, Denmark. *Portrait*, Sven Türck (1897-1954).

Take Matters into Your Own Hands
Reprinted with permission. Department of Maps, Prints and Photographs, The Royal Library, Denmark. *Romance. Kissing on a picnic*, Sven Türck (1897-1954).

Reawaken Your Youth
Reprinted with permission. Department of Maps, Prints and Photographs, The Royal Library, Denmark. *Young people at the beach*, Sven Türck (1897-1954).

Sit in Silence, Alone
Courtesy of the Library of the London School of Economics & Political Science. *Student reading in the Shaw Library, 1964.* IMAGELIBRARY/157.

Draw Close to those Nearest and Dearest
Courtesy of Powerhouse Museum Collection, Thomas Lennon Photographic Archive Collection. *Palmer's Mystery Hike No. 2.*, 10 July 1932. Registration number 94/63/1-48/7.

Don't Mind Being Eccentric
Courtesy of Powerhouse Museum Collection, Thomas Lennon Photographic Archive Collection. *Portrait of strongman Don Athaldo*, 21 November 1936. Registration number 94/63/1-58/13.

Fall in love with Something New
Reprinted with permission. National Library of Ireland. *Goat*, 1964. NLI Ref.: WIL 2[11].

Dive in Deep
Courtesy of the Library of Congress, Prints & Photographs Division, George Grantham Bain Collection, LC-B2- 2819-2. *F.A. Mullen – diving (LOC)*, Bain News Service, publisher, 1913 August 26 (date created or published later by Bain).

FRESH LIME AND JASMINE TEA (METRIC)
3 limes
710 milliliters limeade, chilled
480 milliliters brewed jasmine green tea, chilled
240 milliliters cold water
2 teaspoons finely grated zest plus ¼ cup (2 ounces)
freshly squeezed lime juice from about 4 limes, Ice
cubes, Sugar

ETIQUETTE LIST
Illustrated Text Joy Kim

BACK COVER QUOTE
Ralph Waldo Emerson, "Man the Reformer: A Lecture read before the Mechanics' Apprentices' Library Association, Boston, January 25, 1841" *Essays and Lectures*, ed. Joel Porte (New York: The Library of America, 1983), 144.

ENDNOTES
1 Ariele Alasko, interview by Jennifer Causey, *The Makers Project*, http://www.themakersproject.com/ARIELE-ALASKO, image 15.

2 Laurice Elehwany, *My Girl*, directed by Howard Zieff (1991; Columbia TriStar Home Entertainment, 2005), DVD.

3 Walt Whitman, "Song of the Open Road," *Leaves of Grass* (New York: Doubleday, Doran & Co., Inc., 1940), 3–14.

4 Alice McDermott, *Charming Billy* (New York: Farrar, Straus and Giroux, 1998), 3–6.

THANKS TO OUR DINNER PARTNERS

LOS ANGELES
Apolis: Common Gallery
Brakeman Brewery
Cookbook LA
Casa de Perrin
Greenbar Collective
Handsome Coffee Roasters
Leo Patrone
Moon Juice
Paper & Type
Paper Palate
Peddler's Creamery
Rachel Craven Textiles
TACT Events
Three Sticks Winery
Twig & Twine Design
West Elm
YEAH! Rentals

TORONTO
Bellwoods Brewery
Coriander Girl
Domestic Curator
Fresh City Farms
Herriott Grace
HOI BO Studio
Kipos
La Merceria
Melinda Josie
Mjölk
Silverplate Press
Soma Chocolatemaker
Steven Alan
Stoney Lake Baking Co.
West Elm
Whole Foods
Your Time Boutique

PARIS
Clément Pascal
Rubi Jones
Tifamade

WWW.KINFOLKMAG.COM

KEEP IN TOUCH